EASY START

Kim's little friend

Series editor: Keith Gaines

Illustrated by Margaret de Souza

Nelson

This is Kim's little friend.

"How old is he?"
said Kim.

"He is one,"
said his Mum.

"Can he read?"

said Kim.

"No, he can't read,"

said his Mum.

"He is too small to read."

"Can he run?"

said Kim.

"No, he can't run,"

said his Dad.

"He is too small to run."

"Can he eat an apple?"

said Kim.

"No, he can't eat an apple,"
said his Mum.
"He is too small to eat an apple."

"Can he play a game with us?"
said Kim.

"No, he can't play a game
with you," said his Dad.
"He is too small to play a game."

"What can he do?"
said Kim.

"He can crawl,"

said his Mum and Dad.